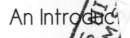

An Introduction to Coping with Health Anxiety

2nd Edition

Brenda Hogan
and
Charles Young

ROBINSON

ROBINSON

First published in Great Britain in 2007 by Robinson,
an imprint of Constable & Robinson Ltd

This edition published in 2017 by Robinson

3 5 7 9 10 8 6 4 2

A CIP catalogue record for this book
is available from the British Library.

Important note
This book is not intended as a substitute for medical advice or treatment.
Any person with a condition requiring medical attention should
consult a qualified medical practitioner or suitable therapist.

ISBN: 978-1-47213-851-4

Typeset in Bembo by Initial Typesetting Services, Edinburgh
Printed and bound in Great Britain by
CPI Group (UK) Ltd, Croydon CR0 4YY

Papers used by Robinson are from well-managed forests
and other responsible sources.

MIX
Paper from
responsible sources
FSC® C104740
www.fsc.org

Robinson
An imprint of
Little, Brown Book Group
Carmelite House
50 Victoria Embankment
London EC4Y 0DZ

An Hachette UK Company
www.hachette.co.uk

www.littlebrown.co.uk

Contents

About This Book

Most of us worry about our health from time to time but generally these worries don't last very long and don't interfere with our lives. Unfortunately, for some of us the worries don't disappear so easily and can become very distressing. Usually, these people are worried that they have a serious illness, and this worry persists even when their doctors have told them otherwise. Worrying like this can cause intense anxiety, feelings of panic, and a feeling that the worry is 'taking over my life'.

You may have heard the term 'hypochondriac' used to describe people who are always worrying that they have something wrong with them or that they have a serious medical condition when they don't. Many people believe that 'hypochondriacs' don't have any real symptoms, and in fact the problem is 'all in the mind'. However, healthcare workers now know that the vast majority of people with health anxiety do have real physical symptoms.

If you worry excessively about your health, this book will help you understand your health anxiety and what keeps it going. Part 1 describes what health anxiety is and Part 2 gives you some guidelines about what you can do to lower the anxiety associated with your health. You'll learn ways to take control of your thoughts and behaviour so you can cope better with your anxiety and get back to living a normal life.

As it's helpful to write things down, Part 2 of the book contains several exercises for you to do, with worked examples to guide you. It's a good idea to get a notebook before you begin to work through these, so that you can keep a record of your thoughts, feelings and progress as suggested in the various exercises.

Brenda Hogan and Charles Young

Part 1: ABOUT HEALTH ANXIETY

1

What is Health Anxiety?

Health anxiety is an intense worry about your health, usually to the point where it makes you feel very distressed and interferes with day-to-day living. You may be convinced you have a serious illness, even though your doctor hasn't diagnosed one.

- Are you preoccupied with worry about having a serious disease and with physical symptoms that you believe may be related to this disease?
- Does the fear continue despite reassurance from your doctor?
- Is there a part of you that realises that your fear may not be 100 per cent reasonable?

If you answered yes to any or all of these questions, you may have a problem with health anxiety.

This chapter sets out the common symptoms and kinds of thinking and behaviour you may have if you have health anxiety.

Physical symptoms

There's a huge variety in the types of physical symptoms you may have, but some of the most common include:

- Chest pain
- General aches and pains
- Palpitations (your heart 'skips a beat' or 'flutters')
- Trembling
- Numbness
- Tightness in the throat
- Rapid heart rate
- Sweating
- Headaches
- Tingling

Some of you may notice a physical change in your body – for example, a lump or a skin blemish.

Kinds of thinking and behaviour

Misinterpretation of normal body sensations

This is the most important aspect of health anxiety: You may believe that a harmless physical symptom like chest pain, headaches or a lump means you have a very serious medical problem.

If you think you have a serious illness, you're likely to become anxious. As you become more anxious, you experience physical symptoms of anxiety – such as an increased heart rate, palpitations (the heart 'fluttering' or 'skipping a beat'), sweating, trembling, muscle tension, light-headedness, tingling sensations, chest pain, difficulty breathing, and so on. These in turn can be misinterpreted as being symptoms of a serious illness.

Worry about symptoms and illness

Worrying about the physical symptoms and about the possibility of serious and life-threatening disease gets worse. You may worry that you won't be able to cope with the effects of serious illness. Not surprisingly, this increases your levels of anxiety.

You may have thoughts or worries such as:

- A sore on my skin means I have skin cancer
- This headache is a sign I might have a brain tumour
- My heart fluttering is a sign I have heart disease or I'm having a heart attack
- Difficulty swallowing is a sign of throat cancer

There are many other kinds of thoughts or worries that bother people with health anxiety. Usually there is concern about a specific physical symptom(s) or sensation(s) and that this symptom is a sign of a very serious health problem.

Increased focus on the body and checking

When you're worried that you may have a serious illness, you may find that you begin to focus on your body more. It's common to be preoccupied with physical symptoms and to be repeatedly checking the body for any physical changes or signs of illness.

Seeking reassurance from doctors and nurses

People with health anxiety often make appointments to see their doctor and ask for medical examinations, hoping to ease their fears. They may visit their GP more frequently and ask to see different doctors for a second or third opinion. Alternatively, some people avoid consulting their doctors because they're frightened that a medical examination will confirm their worst fears.

Seeking reassurance from family and friends

If you have health anxiety you may find yourself mentioning your symptoms to family and friends and asking them what they think about your health, in the hope that they'll tell you everything is all right.

Spending time finding out about illness

Some people are so concerned about the possibility of being ill that they read a lot about illnesses and check out their symptoms in medical encyclopedias, in magazine articles, or on the Internet. Internet search engines are increasingly used as a source of health information. When people search for such information, they are usually hoping that they will be reassured that they do not have a life-threatening illness and will have no need to worry.

Avoiding things to do with illness

Quite frequently, people with health anxiety will stop watching TV programmes or reading newspapers or magazines that might mention the illness they're afraid of. Or they even stop talking about it. People try not to think about the illness that frightens them most to try to avoid being anxious.

Other kinds of avoidance

Many people stop doing things that produce the symptom they are worried about, or give up things they fear may put their health at further risk. They may avoid walking, sports and other forms of exercise. Some people go to bed or sit down whenever they notice a physical symptom.

Mary's story

Mary is 36 and works full-time as a physio-therapist. She gave up smoking a few years ago. Over the past six months she has become more and more concerned that she may have lung cancer. The anxiety about her physical health seemed to begin around the time she had a chest cold that coincided with an increase in stress at work, as her list of patients was growing quite long.

As Mary recovered from the chest cold, she became concerned about a lingering cough. Then she noticed that she was getting pains in her chest. At other times she noticed that it was becoming more difficult to breathe easily. She went to her GP, who told her not to worry. When her symptoms did not improve, she returned to her GP, who did some tests. When the results of the tests came back, her GP told her that she was fine. She felt better for a few weeks and the cough went away, but then the pains and the breathing difficulties returned.

This worried Mary more, and she started to read about the symptoms of lung cancer on the Internet. She found that this made her much more anxious; she couldn't stop thinking about her chest pain and breathing difficulties, and spent a lot of time worrying that she had cancer. She began to avoid reading about cancer in magazines, and would turn off the television if she suspected that cancer might be discussed on a programme she was watching.

Mary returned to the doctor several times; at the time this seemed to give her some relief, but a few days after each visit, the doubts started to creep back. She began asking her husband whether he thought she had lung cancer. She kept a very close eye on her symptoms. She would sit or lie down whenever she noticed chest pain or breathing difficulties. She stopped exercising, and went out less and less. Her level of distress increased as her worries about her health continued to bother her.

Mary had several of the features of health anxiety we talked about at the beginning of this chapter:

- She had physical symptoms (cough, chest pain, difficulty breathing) and worried a lot about them.
- She was afraid that her physical symptoms were a sign that she had a serious medical problem – lung cancer.
- She focused on her physical symptoms and kept a check on them.
- She sought reassurance from her GP and from her husband.
- At first she looked for information about lung cancer on the Internet, but when she discovered that this increased her anxiety, she started to avoid any mention of cancer at all.
- She stopped doing anything that she thought might endanger her health or make her symptoms worse, and would sit or lie down every time she noticed the physical symptoms.

2

Who Develops Health Anxiety and Why?

What triggers health anxiety?

There are many possible reasons why you might become over-anxious about your health. Some of you may have always been 'worriers' or sensitive to feelings of anxiety. It's common for people to start worrying about their health when they feel under a lot of stress (even when the stress has nothing to do with health).

Health anxiety may be triggered when someone you know becomes seriously ill. If this is the case for you, you may find yourself worrying that you have the same illness as that person.

Your health anxiety may have begun after you read or heard about a serious illness and then you started to monitor or check your body for signs of this illness.

Another possibility is that you may have started to worry excessively about your health after you had some sort of illness – this becomes a problem when the worry continues even though your doctor has told you that you have been successfully treated.

People sometimes find that their health anxiety comes and goes over many years. Flare-ups sometimes coincide with important life milestones, such as starting a new career, having children or buying a new home. While these can be stressful on their own, they may also prompt people to think about their futures and to ask themselves what might go wrong.

What illnesses do people worry about?

People with health anxiety tend to worry about certain diseases more than others. It's no surprise that the illnesses causing the most anxiety are the most frightening ones – cancer, heart disease and brain problems are good examples. Whenever a particular disease gets a lot of media attention, lots of people worry that they have it.

3

What Keeps Health Anxiety Going?

Some of the things you may be doing to cope with health anxiety may actually keep the anxiety going. Remember the list of ways of thinking and behaving associated with health anxiety (pages 6–10)? Many of these are things people do in an effort to cope with their excessive worrying about their health. But do they work? Some, if not all, of these are helpful in the short term – that is, they reduce anxiety for the time being. That's why people use them! Unfortunately, in the long term, they actually keep the problem going.

Worrying about symptoms and illness

Once you start feeling anxious about your health, it can seem very difficult to stop worrying. You may be worrying about the actual symptoms you're experiencing – Is it getting worse? Better? How is it today compared to yesterday? – as well as worrying about whether they're a sign of a serious health problem. You may also be worrying if you'll be able to cope with a serious illness, and may imagine yourself terminally ill, feeling extremely physically unwell and emotionally unable to cope. You may also imagine what would happen to your loved ones if you were to become seriously ill. Worrying about symptoms and illness leads to increased levels of anxiety. And, as we saw in Chapter 1, increased anxiety, accompanied by the physical symptoms that go with anxiety, causes even more worry, leading to a vicious circle of anxiety and worry.

Think back to Mary, whose case we looked at in Chapter 1. Let's suppose that Mary noticed chest pain, which made her start thinking, 'Maybe this means I have lung cancer.' This led to her feeling anxious and this anxiety produced lots of physical changes. Mary experienced chest pain and short-ness of breath as a result of her anxiety; but for her these symptoms were further proof that she had lung cancer. Not surprisingly, this made her more anxious – and so the vicious circle continued.

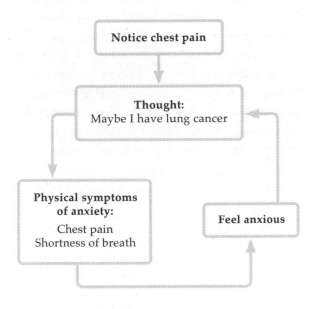

Worry and superstitious beliefs

Sometimes people who struggle with health anxiety believe that worrying will do some good. They become superstitious about it – for example, they might think 'If I worry I can protect myself from getting ill' or 'If I stop worrying, I'll tempt fate'. These kinds of belief about worry can make it difficult to stop worrying, and therefore feed into the vicious circle of anxiety and worry.

Increased focus on the body and checking

Misinterpreting normal everyday changes

People with health anxiety tend to spend a lot of time focusing on the feelings in their body. The result of this is that they notice lots of sensations that most people pay very little attention to. These sensations are perfectly normal, but can easily be misinterpreted.

> Try this experiment: Close your eyes for one minute. While your eyes are closed, focus your attention on your feet – what they feel like, every sensation that you experience from the ankles down. After one minute, open your eyes. What did you notice? With all of your attention focused on your feet, you may have noticed all sorts of things you hadn't been paying any attention to before-hand. You may have felt your toes touching each other, or the sensation of your shoes or the soles of your feet touching the floor,

or sensations of temperature (warm or cool). These sensations were there all along! They did not just suddenly start happening because you were paying attention. Later, when you start focusing on something else, these symptoms will again fade into the background and go unnoticed.

The point of this experiment is to demonstrate that when you focus on your body and the physical sensations you are experiencing, you notice all sorts of things – but these sensations are normal and are there all along.

Constant checking of physical symptoms may seem like a good idea – that way, you'll notice even a small change in the severity or intensity of a physical sensation, and therefore you'll detect potential problems. But while generally it's a good idea to be aware of how you are doing physically, it's actually not helpful to pay close attention to your body at all times. This is because your body naturally changes over the course of the day, as well as over longer periods of time. This is entirely normal. So noticing every tiny change provides very little useful information.

Feeding the vicious circle of anxiety

On top of this, constantly monitoring physical symptoms can make you very sensitive to any physical change or sensation, so you may discover things that you have never noticed before, and this may also increase your worry. As worry increases, so does anxiety, and then anxiety may make the physical changes and symptoms get worse; and as this happens, you'll be checking even more. In other words, focusing too much on your body feeds into the vicious circle of health anxiety.

Checking that makes symptoms worse

Some people do more than just a 'mental scan' of their body – in addition, they may poke and prod themselves to check for changes, or do things like swallow again and again to assess the severity of throat pain or tightness. Just like focusing on the body mentally, this sort of behaviour keeps your attention on the symptom and means that you will notice even the smallest change, which will make you even more worried and anxious.

Checking in this way can also make your health anxiety worse by aggravating the symptom you are worrying about. For example, imagine repeatedly touching and pressing on one spot on your arm. After a while, your arm would start to hurt – even if it didn't hurt in the first place. Keep touching and prodding, and the skin may turn red and it may feel swollen. In this case, you would have produced the symptom that you were afraid of!

Again, checking feeds into a vicious circle.

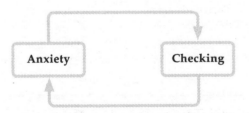

Seeking reassurance

People with health anxiety are likely to seek re-assurance about their health from their doctors, and they sometimes even check with their family and friends. In most cases, they are told that nothing is wrong. This quickly makes them feel better. But the reassurance doesn't last. What happens in the long term? Reassurance tends to encourage pre-occupation with health.

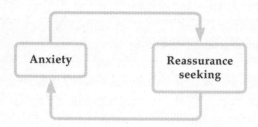

Many people want to feel absolutely certain that they don't have a serious illness. But it is impossible to ever be 100 per cent certain – there are often more tests that can be done and more specialists you can consult. If you are trying to prove once and for all that you don't have and will never get a disease, you are setting yourself an endless and probably fruitless task that's going to make you feel more and more anxious.

Spending time finding out about illness

Some people with health anxiety read a lot about the illness they're worried about (or illness in general) and look up their 'symptoms' in a medical book, on the Internet, or in magazines. Searching for health information on the Internet, in particular, is such a common activity and so strongly associated with increased health anxiety that it has been called 'cyberchondria'. Finding out about illnesses can be a problem for several reasons. First, it is another example of paying too much attention to your health. Reading about illness can make you think even more about your body, and notice even more sensations. And if you keep looking, you are bound to find something about a symptom you have. Even though the symptom is not due to you being seriously ill, you may start worrying that you have the illness in question. The more attention you pay to that symptom, the more you worry … and so on.

Furthermore, when you search on the Internet about non-specific symptoms, such as having a cough or headache, you will be exposed to a disproportionately large amount of information on serious life-threatening illnesses. Research shows that people progress from searching about common symptoms to much less common, serious illnesses. This can make these worst-case scenarios seem much more likely than they really are, and the result is that you are much more likely to interpret benign symptoms as a sign of a much more sinister and catastrophic illness.

Another problem is that sometimes people read up on illnesses as a way of telling themselves that they are not ill. This does not work! We have already talked about how reassurance seeking encourages a preoccupation with your health and increases your exposure to the rare and serious diseases, which keeps anxiety going in the long term. In addition to this, information that you will find on the Internet is often unreliable and contradictory, which may cause you to doubt any sound advice that you have already been given by your doctor. No wonder that most people who spend time finding out about illness don't end up feeling reassured at all, even in the short term – instead, they feel much more anxious.

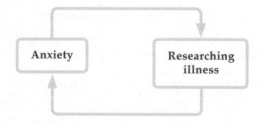

Avoiding information about illness

While many look for information about the diseases they dread, some people do the opposite and stop watching programmes on TV or reading articles in magazines or newspapers about the illness they're most afraid of. Other people avoid talking about the illness. This kind of avoidance can have the short-term effect of reducing worrying thoughts. But what happens in the long term? The worries are still there. Avoidance does not make you think in a realistic way about your health, and until you can do that, the anxiety won't go away.

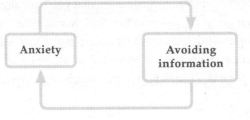

Avoiding physical activity

Some people avoid physical activities as a way of protecting themselves from illness; they will lie down every time they notice a symptom. Not only does this kind of behaviour make your life less enjoyable and interesting, it also makes you less physically fit. As your fitness declines, you become more likely to tire quickly from any sort of exercise, and may tend to lose your breath more easily. This may end up increasing your worries about your health, and lead to you reducing what you do even more. This is another example of a strategy to cope with health anxiety that makes the situation even worse.

Conclusion

To sum up: many of the strategies you use to cope with anxiety about your health may actually be making your anxiety worse and keeping the problem going.

Do your existing coping strategies really work?

You started using these strategies for a reason: they work in the short term. But what about the long term?

You have probably been trying quite a few of these strategies to try to ease your anxiety about your health. Have they been helpful, or have they actually been making matters worse? One way to find out is to make a list of all of the things you've done to try to help yourself feel better. Now make some notes about how helpful these strategies have been in terms of reducing your anxiety or helping you cope. Then write down how they have not been helpful and what problems they've caused you. Consider the effect of these strategies on your anxiety in the long term. Have they worked?

Let's look at Mary's coping strategies:

How I have tried to reduce anxiety about my health	How this strategy has been helpful	How this strategy has not been helpful
Going to the doctor	Made me feel better for a little while.	I felt anxious again a few days later. I end up going to the doctor a lot. And I still feel anxious!
Talking about the symptoms with my husband	This can make me feel better for a little while.	The reassurance doesn't last long – then I just want to talk to him about it again. He is starting to get a bit fed up with me.

Looking up symptoms on the Internet	I don't think this was helpful at all! It made me feel very frightened.	Looking up symptoms on the Internet made me more worried and anxious.
Avoiding TV programmes and magazine articles about cancer	If I don't watch these programmes or read about cancer, I don't feel as anxious.	I'm still really worried about my health.
Avoiding exercise	I don't get so anxious if I don't feel so short of breath.	I'm getting less fit, which means that I end up feeling short of breath more easily. I end up getting anxious. Also, exercise helps me manage my stress, and I have noticed that I am much more stressed since I started to avoid exercise.

Now it's your turn. On a blank sheet of paper, in your notebook, or on your computer or smartphone, copy out the three column headings in the table on the previous page and list your own strategies; then note how they have helped or not in managing your health anxiety.

After doing this exercise, you'll probably see that most or perhaps all of the things you are currently doing to try to cope with your health anxiety are in fact keeping the problem going. So what is a better way to cope? Part 2 of this book sets out some guidelines and exercises to help you decrease your anxiety about your health in the long term.

Part 2: COPING WITH HEALTH ANXIETY

4

What Can You Do to Get Rid of Health Anxiety?

There are many things you can do to reduce health anxiety; however, there's no magic wand that will make your anxiety disappear overnight. Coping with health anxiety is going to take a lot of effort on your part, and you will need to start making changes to the ways in which you're thinking and the ways in which you're behaving. These changes will in time help you become less preoccupied and worried about your health.

A problem with worry, not a problem with health

While you thought your problem was with your health, your health is probably fine. The real problem is more likely to be that you are very worried about your health! Not only is the worry making you feel anxious, it is probably leading you to use coping strategies that are actually making the problem worse. So, it's a good idea to move the focus away from whether or not you have a disease and towards the worry itself.

You may be having a few thoughts that are making you feel a bit hesitant about getting rid of health anxiety – thoughts like 'What if something is really wrong with me and the doctors just haven't discovered it yet?' The truth is that no one can say with complete certainty that nothing is wrong with you. There's always a chance that you may develop illness at some point in your life. But the chance of this may be much less than you are imagining.

So, if your doctor has told you that nothing is wrong at the moment, then you may very well find the methods described in this book helpful. You may like to approach the strategies outlined here as a series of experiments. If they work, that's great; you'll feel much better. If not, you always have the option of resuming your old ways of dealing with the anxiety. You've got nothing to lose!

The following chapters outline a variety of ways you can learn to manage your anxiety about your health.

5

Assessing Where You Are Now

Keeping a diary of thoughts and behaviour

While you may realise that you are indeed using
many of the unhelpful strategies identified in
Chapter 3, you may be a bit unsure about how
frequently you are using them or which ones are
causing you the most trouble. It can be very useful
to keep a diary for a few weeks to keep track of your
thoughts and behaviour related to health anxiety.

Keep your eyes open for unhelpful strategies that
you weren't previously aware you were using. The
diary can help you get a much more accurate picture
of what you are doing to keep your health anxiety
going. Once this is clear in your mind, you'll be in
a better position to know what to focus on to get
over this problem.

There's a sample diary below. Feel free to make
copies of this to help you keep track of your symptoms over the next few weeks. After a couple of

weeks, look back over your diary entries – this will help you to spot which kinds of thoughts and behaviours you use most often.

As you work through the rest of this manual and begin to use better ways of coping with health anxiety, it's a good idea to continue with the diary so that you can check reductions in your anxiety-related thoughts and behaviours and see the effect on your overall level of anxiety.

Daily diary for health anxiety

Look at the diary below. Make a copy of it in your notebook or on your computer or smartphone to fill in each day over the next few weeks to keep track of your health anxiety and the strategies you've been using to cope with it. Record the physical symptoms that concern you and describe your worrying thoughts. Rate how often these thoughts occur (use a 0–10 scale, where 0 represents not at all and 10 represents almost all of the time). Also, make a note of what strategies you use to try to help your anxiety, as well as how often you use these strategies (sometimes it may be easier to use the 0–10 scale rather than counting the number of times). Finally, rate your anxiety level for each day, using a 0–10 scale where 0 represents no anxiety at all and 10 represents very intense anxiety.

Date	
Physical symptom	
Worrying thoughts (describe and rate frequency on a 0–10 scale)	
Focus on body (rate frequency on a 0–10 scale)	

Checking (make a note of what you did as well as how many times you checked)	
Reassurance-seeking (from doctors or friends/family) (make a note of what kind of reassurance-seeking you used as well as how many times you used it)	
Searching for health information on the Internet or elsewhere (make a note of what information you were searching for and where you looked for it)	

Avoidance (make a note of any avoidance and rate frequency on a 0–10 scale)	
Overall anxiety (rate on a 0–10 scale)	

6

Dealing with Worry about Symptoms and Illness

Identifying worrying thoughts

The very first step is to work out what exactly your worries are. People who fret about their health may have all kinds of worries. Some examples from Mary's case are listed below:

- I'm having chest pain again. I'm sure it's not getting any better.
- My breathing seems difficult. When I try to breathe deeply, I don't seem to be able to fill my lungs. Something must be wrong.
- Maybe I have lung cancer.
- If I do have cancer, I'm sure it will be very advanced and probably incurable.
- I'm going to die a painful death.
- I won't be able to cope with having cancer and with dying.
- What will happen to my husband? How will he cope?

Worrying thoughts: the three main mistakes

Worrying thoughts about health tend to have three main characteristics. People tend to:

- **overestimate** the likelihood that a symptom is a sign of serious illness;

- **overestimate** the severity of any possible illness;

- **underestimate** their ability to cope with potential illness.

It's important to spend some time working out just what kinds of worrying thoughts you are having. Sometimes it's difficult to identify worrying thoughts because they can happen so quickly that you may not notice you are having them. At first, you may have to pay very close attention to what is going through your mind when you start to feel anxious.

Recording your worrying thoughts

It's very useful to keep a record of the thoughts you are having whenever you start feeling worried or anxious about your health. Start by writing down what you were doing or what happened when you first felt anxious – the 'trigger'. Then write down exactly what you were thinking – what was running through your mind when you started to feel anxious – and then jot it down. Next, write down how you felt – your emotions. Anxiety is not the only possibility; for example, you may also feel sad or panicky. Make a note of how strongly you feel the emotion on a 0–10 scale, where 0 represents *not at all* and 10 represents *very strongly*.

Here is an example of a thought record that Mary might have made:

Trigger	What were you thinking about?	How did this make you feel?
Feeling stressed at work	I'm having chest pain again. I'm sure it's not getting any better. My breathing seems difficult. When I try to breathe deeply, I don't seem to be able to fill my lungs. Something must be wrong. Maybe I have lung cancer.	anxious (8) panicky (9) scared (10)

In a notebook, on a sheet of paper or on your computer or smartphone, copy these three headings and below them record your own triggers, thoughts and feelings (with ratings). You may want to keep this record for at least a week or so to get a good idea of what kinds of situations trigger anxious thoughts, what kind of thoughts you are having, and how these thoughts are affecting your emotions.

Challenging our worrying thoughts

The next step is to learn how to challenge your anxious thoughts and begin to think about your symptoms and health in a fairer and realistic way. This section covers five ways that you can do this.

Considering other explanations for your symptoms

Very often, people dismiss the possibility that the physical symptoms or sensations that worry them are due to normal bodily changes or a minor ailment, and instead jump to the conclusion that they are a sign of a very unpleasant or even life-threatening disease. Some other possible causes of physical symptoms and sensations are listed below.

Normal physical changes

Our bodies change every minute of every day. The vast majority of these changes are harmless and are simply the result of our bodies doing their job. Stiff muscles or joints, changes in heart rate, and stomach discomfort are good examples of this kind of change.

Some other changes are part of the natural variations that happen in the human body from time to time: for example, headaches, white marks on the fingernails, skin blemishes, and lumps.

Other changes happen regularly over a period of time, which means they have a relatively predictable schedule. This is particularly so for women, who may notice physical changes as a result of their menstrual cycle, such as headaches, cramping, and tenderness and 'lumpiness' in their breasts.

All of these changes are normal and harmless.

Common and non-serious illness

Sometimes the physical symptoms people worry about are actually the result of widespread and non-serious problems. For example, coughs, fever and sore throats are most often caused by a cold, the flu, or minor allergies. Likewise, blemishes and rashes are generally a sign of minor skin irritation, and stomach discomfort is frequently a result of indigestion.

Physical symptoms of anxiety

Anxiety, as we've already seen, can cause a wide range of physical symptoms. Very often, too, when people get nervous or anxious they begin to 'over-breathe', which means that their breathing becomes fast and shallow. Over-breathing can cause other physical symptoms, such as light-headedness, tingling sensations and changes to your vision. These physical symptoms caused by anxiety and by over-breathing, although uncomfortable, are harmless and do not last long.

Focusing on physical sensations

Many people find that their symptoms increase in severity and/or that they notice the symptoms more when they are focusing on them. When they turn their attention to something else, they stop noticing the symptom or it seems less intense.

Physical fitness

Even if you're very fit, exercise can sometimes cause stiff muscles and aches and pains. But what if you're out of shape? Even small increases in physical activity can cause unpleasant but harmless symptoms, including raised heart rate, tightness in the chest, sweating and muscle pain.

Food and drink

Do you drink a lot of drinks that contain caffeine – tea and cola, as well as coffee? You'll probably feel jittery, your heart may feel like it's racing, and you may even start sweating. And if you don't get the amount of caffeine you're used to, then you may feel tired and shaky, or get a headache. Drinking alcohol can also produce physical changes, including headaches, nausea and changes in heart rate, as well as the typical effects of intoxication. And, of course, you may suffer the physical effects of a hangover. Eating too little or too much can also produce uncomfortable physical sensations.

Sleep

Too little or too much sleep can produce physical changes, including fatigue, drowsiness and headaches.

In summary, there are many possible explanations for physical symptoms and sensations. In your notebook, on a sheet of paper, or on your computer or smartphone, write down every other possible explanation you can think of for the physical sensation(s) or symptom(s) you've been worried about.

Now consider: how likely is it that the symptom or sensation you're concerned about is due to serious illness? How likely is it that it is due to one of the other (much less scary) explanations listed above?

This leads on to the next step, which is learning to be more fair and realistic when estimating the likelihood of serious illness.

Correctly estimating the probability of serious illness

First, think about how strongly you believe at the moment that the physical symptoms or sensations you experience are a sign of a serious disease. Estimate the probability as a percentage, that is, using a scale of 0 (no chance at all) to 100 (definitely). Write it down:

Looking at all the possible causes

One way to make a more realistic assessment of this likelihood is to think about all the other possible causes of that particular symptom or sensation. You have already started working on this – remember the list of 'other explanations' you made in the previous section.

For example, if you were worried that a headache was a sign that you had a brain tumour, you would write down every other possible cause of a headache that you could think of – things like:

- muscle tension
- anxiety
- menstrual cycle

- normal physical change or variation
- blocked sinuses
- too much time on the computer
- not enough sleep the last few nights
- skipped lunch
- one too many glasses of wine last night

... and so on.

Using your notebook, a piece of paper, or your computer or smartphone, write down the symptom that is bothering you, what you think this means is wrong with you, and all other possible causes of the symptom you can think of. The more possibilities you can think of, the better!

Now that you have listed all of the other possible causes of the physical symptom or sensation you are worried about, it's time to estimate the probability of each possible cause.

A handy way to do this is to use a pie chart. Start with the first item on your list of all other possible causes of the physical symptom or sensation. What is the chance that the physical symptom is due to this cause? Give it a percentage chance (between 0 and 100) and give it about that portion of the pie chart. For example, if you thought that there was about a 20 per cent chance that your headache was due to muscle tension, then you'd start your pie chart like this:

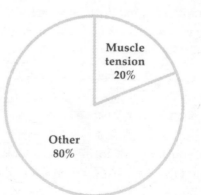

Then move on to the next item on your list and estimate the chance that your symptom is due to that cause, and add it to your pie chart, where it will take up a piece of the big section marked 'Other' in the first chart. Keep going through all of the possible causes of your symptom, adding each one to the pie chart, until you have something that looks like this:

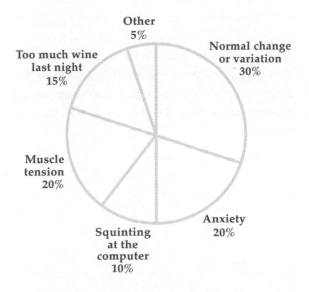

When you have got to this point, look carefully at your pie chart. Now think about the serious health problem you were worried about. Given the likelihood of all the other causes, how would you now rate the chance that the physical symptom or sensation you are worried about is due to that serious health problem? Remember, you have to take into account the likelihood of all the other causes; all you have left is the space for 'other'. So your finished chart might look like this:

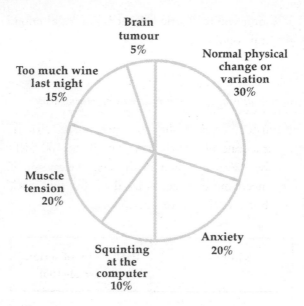

All you need to do to start your own pie chart is to draw a circle on a sheet of paper, in your notebook, or on your computer or smartphone, leaving space around it to write all the various possibilities.

When you've finished this exercise, it's time to rethink the likelihood that the physical symptom or sensation you're worried about is due to a serious medical condition.

How likely is it that the physical symptom you are worried about is a sign of a very serious health problem?

Estimate the probability as a percentage, that is, using a scale of 0 (no chance at all) to 100 (definitely). Write it down in the table below, or, if you need more space, copy the table into your notebook, computer or smartphone.

Symptoms	Probability of serious disease (1–100)

Compare this to your original rating.

Putting the symptom or sensation in context

There are other ways to make a more realistic estimate of the likelihood that a physical symptom or sensation is due to serious illness. Ask yourself the following questions:

What is the physical symptom you are worried about?

Now think about the city, town or village where you live. How many people in the place where you live do you think had a similar symptom this morning?

How many people still had this symptom by the evening?

How many people will still have the symptom tomorrow?

How many people will still have the symptom a week from now?

How many people will go to the doctor?

How many people will be sent for medical tests?

How many people are told the problem is serious?

How many people are successfully treated?

How many people does that leave?

Look at your original number and compare it to the number of people left, unsuccessfully treated. What are the odds?

Example

Mary lived in Cambridge and she estimated that two thousand people woke up with chest pain this morning. She thought that about one thousand people still had chest pain that evening, five hundred the next morning, and fifty still had it a week later. She estimated that thirty people went to the doctor and ten were sent for tests. Of the people sent for tests, she guessed that about three were told it was serious, and one was successfully treated. That left two people – two people out of the original two thousand who had chest pain. This is a very small proportion of people! But Mary had originally jumped to the conclusion that her chest pain very likely meant that she had a serious illness.

After you have completed the exercise, ask yourself again:

How likely is it that the physical symptoms you are worried about is a sign of a very serious health problem? Estimate the probability as a percentage, that is, using a scale of 0 (no chance at all) to 100 (definitely). Write it down in the table below, or, if you need more space, copy the table into your notebook or onto your computer or smartphone.

Symptoms	Probability of serious disease (1–100)

Compare this number with the original rating.

Weighing the evidence

If you're going to learn to think about your health in a fair and realistic way, then it's important to consider all of the evidence.

You can start by writing down all the evidence that indicates that you are seriously ill. That's one side of the story – and the one you usually pay most attention to!

Now it's time to consider the other side of the story. Ask yourself whether the symptoms could be caused by something else. Write down all the other possible explanations of your symptoms, as well as any other evidence you can think of that would suggest that you're not seriously ill. When you have put all this down, review the facts. Pretend that you are a judge reviewing the evidence. What do you think – which set of evidence is the most convincing? Give each side of the case a percentage rating (1–100), according to how likely you think each explanation is.

Here's Mary's example:

Evidence that I am seriously ill	Evidence that I am not seriously ill
I have chest pain. (10%)	I'm very stressed at the moment – maybe that's causing the chest pain.
	The chest pain goes away if I lie down or focus on breathing deeply – lung cancer pain wouldn't go away so easily.
	My chest pain feels better right after I get reassurance from the doctor. If I really had lung cancer, the symptoms wouldn't get better just because I was reassured!
	Just because cancer was on the news tonight doesn't make it more likely that I have cancer.
	(90%)

After reviewing the evidence, Mary summarised her judgement: *On the basis of the evidence, it's overwhelmingly unlikely that my chest pain is caused by a serious illness.*

In your notebook, on a piece of paper, or on your computer or smartphone, make two column headings, 'Evidence that I am seriously ill' and 'Evidence that I'm not seriously ill' and make a list under each.

When you have reviewed the evidence, what's your conclusion? Write it below your list of evidence, beginning 'On the basis of the evidence ...'

Remember that it is also important to address negative thoughts you may be having about your ability to cope. It is common for people with health anxiety to think about or imagine catastrophic outcomes, such as dying slow and painful deaths due to their feared disease, and to have thoughts such as 'I would never be able to cope' or 'My family will not be able to cope'. Imagining the emotional consequences of serious illness can also be very anxiety provoking. The error in this kind of thinking is underestimating your (or your friends or family's) ability to cope with difficult and challenging situations. You can help deal with this kind of unhelpful thinking by using the same strategy of weighing the evidence. What evidence do you have that you will not be able to cope? What evidence do you have that you would be able to cope? Think back to challenges you have faced in the past, big or small. What did you do? How did you get through them? Did you come out the other side? What kinds of things have you done to deal with challenging situations you have encountered in the past? Given all of this information, what makes you think you can't cope with any health challenges you might face?

Practising fair and realistic thinking

Challenging negative thoughts

Worrying thoughts that pop into our heads tend to be negative and distorted, and you can learn to identify and challenge them.

Challenging negative thinking patterns requires you to step back and look at the situation from outside. You'll need to examine the evidence for your initial anxious thoughts and decide whether these thoughts are fair and realistic. If you decide – on the basis of objective evidence, remember – that they aren't, you'll then try to come up with a more fair and realistic thought – again, based on the evidence, not on distorted thinking.

Learning to challenge negative thoughts and replace them with more fair and realistic thoughts isn't easy – it takes practice. At first, you'll probably find it difficult, but most people say that it gets much easier the more they do it. People also usually find that the exercise of challenging unhelpful anxious thoughts gets more effective the more they do it.

Using a thought record

Thought challenging is easier if you use a step-by-step process. The thought record on page 64 is set up to help you do this. The first few steps are similar to what you've already done. First, make a note of what triggered your feelings of anxiety – whatever you were doing when you started feeling anxious. Next, write down the thoughts that seem to be related to how you feel. Then record your emotion on a scale of 0 to 10, where 0 is completely calm and 10 is very intense feeling.

The next step is the most important: think about the situation and try to come up with a more fair and realistic alternative thought.

You can use some of the strategies you've already learned to help you with this. For example, think about other explanations for your symptoms and try to assess the probability of serious disease more realistically. Weighing the evidence is another very useful tactic. This process is similar to having an argument with yourself – fight back against your anxious thinking by giving yourself a chance to think fairly and realistically.

Finally, reassess your emotion after coming up with some alternate, more rational, ways of thinking.

On page 64 you will find an example of a completed thought record based on Mary's case.

It can be quite difficult to come up with fair and realistic alternatives to your anxious thoughts, especially when you first begin to use the thought-challenging method. As mentioned previously, it can be very useful to use some of the strategies you've already learned. If you're still having trouble, you might want to ask yourself some of these questions:

- What evidence do I have for this thought? What about evidence that does not support this thought? On the basis of this evidence, what would be a more fair and realistic thought?
- Am I jumping to conclusions?
- Could my symptoms be related to something else besides illness? Maybe there are other possibilities. What are they?
- Am I over-estimating the risk of a serious illness? If so, how so?
- What's a less extreme way of looking at this situation?
- What's the effect of believing this thought? What would be the effect of changing my thinking?
- If I were less anxious about this problem, what would I say to myself?
- What would I tell a friend who had this worrying thought?
- What would a good friend tell me if he or

Trigger	What were you thinking about?	How did you feel? (rate 0–10)	What would be a more fair and realistic way of thinking about this?	How do you feel now? (rate 0–10)
Feeling stressed at work	I'm having chest pain again. I'm sure it's not getting any better.	Anxious (8)	This chest pain is probably caused by anxiety. I know that anxiety causes chest pain and I've been really stressed out lately. That's probably why it's not getting better.	Anxious (4)
	My breathing seems difficult. When I try to breathe deeply, I don't seem to be able to fill my lungs. Something must be wrong.	Panicky (9)	My breathing is getting more difficult as I get more anxious. I need to relax my muscles and slow down my breathing.	Panicky (3)
	Maybe I have lung cancer	Scared (10)	My breathing is normal when I'm feeling calmer and when I'm thinking	Scared (5)

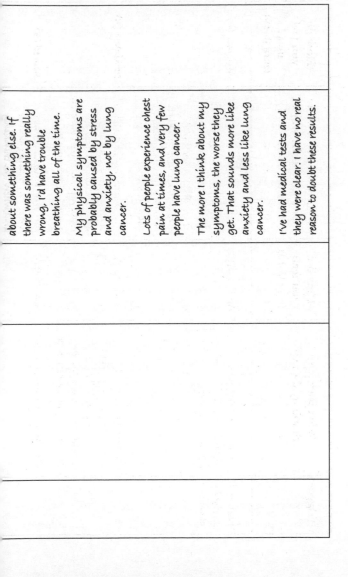

about something else. If there was something really wrong, I'd have trouble breathing all of the time.

My physical symptoms are probably caused by stress and anxiety, not by lung cancer.

Lots of people experience chest pain at times, and very few people have lung cancer.

The more I think about my symptoms, the worse they get. That sounds more like anxiety and less like lung cancer.

I've had medical tests and they were clear. I have no real reason to doubt these results.

she knew about my thought? What evidence would they point out to me that does not support this thought?

- What are all the reasons I shouldn't be worried about my health? (For example, do I have any evidence that I'm healthy?)
- Am I focusing too much on information that fits in with my worries and not believing evidence that I'm healthy?
- Am I questioning my doctor and the medical results even though I've no real reason to do this?

Being realistic about your ability to cope

As we have discussed, sometimes people also worry about how they'd cope if they were seriously ill. They often find themselves thinking things like 'I won't be able to handle a serious illness – I'll fall apart' or 'The pain and suffering will be awful and I won't be able to handle it' or 'I won't be able to cope even though my family will need me to be strong'. Sometimes people also worry about their loved ones' ability to cope, and may have such thoughts as 'I will be such a burden on my wife. She won't be able to handle the stress or be able to cope with the fact that she might lose me.'

It is very important to challenge these thoughts too. When people feel very anxious, they very often under-estimate their ability to cope. Again, think of the evidence about your ability to cope with stressful situations.

Ask yourself these questions:

- Have I successfully managed stressful situations in the past?
- If so, how?
- What kinds of personal strengths or assets can I draw on to help me manage stressful situations now?
- Who can I rely on for support?

You should also be careful not to under-estimate the ability of others to cope. (They might not appreciate it if they knew that you thought they'd fall apart in a crisis!) Do you have any evidence that your loved ones are able to cope with stress? If so, be careful not to disregard this. Instead, use it to develop more fair and rational thoughts.

There is a blank thought record on the next page. Make a copy on a blank sheet of paper, in your notebook or on your computer or smartphone if you need more space, and have a go at challenging your anxious thoughts and coming up with more fair and rational alternatives. Remember, this won't be easy at first – it'll take time and lots of practice. It's a very good idea to keep a daily record of your

Trigger	What were you thinking about?	How did you feel? (rate 0–10)	What would be a more fair and realistic way of thinking about this?	How do you feel now? (rate 0–10)

worrying thoughts and your alternative fair and realistic thoughts. You may want to take a copy of the thought record with you wherever you go, and practise challenging your worrying thoughts as often as you can. Don't stop just as soon as you start to feel better. Continue to practise this for as long as it takes to replace what has usually become a habitual way of anxious thinking with a new habitual way of fair and realistic thinking. For many people, this takes weeks if not months.

Dealing with 'superstitious thinking'

Even though worrying can be a miserable experience, some people do believe that it can be useful. Some of these beliefs can be superstitious in nature, such as 'If I worry about my health, I can protect myself from illness' or 'If I let myself believe I am healthy then I am tempting fate'. Not everyone has superstitious beliefs about worrying; however, for people who do, it can be very difficult to 'let go' of worrying.

In your notebook, on a fresh sheet of paper, or on your computer or smartphone, write down any superstitious beliefs you have about the benefits of worrying.

Unfortunately, these beliefs can convince you that you should be worrying. Not surprisingly, this can just make you worry more. Here is an example of how this works:

Trigger	Superstitious belief about worrying	Increased worry
Headache	'If I let myself believe this is just a normal headache, I will jinx myself. As a result I'll soon find out that something is really wrong.'	I'm worried that the headache is a sign of a brain tumour.

Superstitious beliefs about the benefits of worrying can be a real barrier to reducing worry about your health, because if you believe that worrying is protecting you in some way, you'll not really want to let it go. It's very important to examine your beliefs about worrying and evaluate the evidence for and against these beliefs.

A good place to start is to weigh the advantages and disadvantages of worrying, just as you did when weighing the evidence about your symptoms or sensations. Here's an example:

Advantages of worrying	Disadvantages of worrying
Worrying about my health is what protects me.	Worry makes me anxious and miserable.
If I stop worrying about my health, I'm tempting fate.	I spend too much time worrying – it's interfering with my life. My worries are often unrealistic. Maybe if I stopped worrying, my health would be OK. This would mean that worrying is just wasting my time and making me feel really anxious.

Try filling in a chart like this for yourself, under the headings 'Advantages of worrying' and 'Disadvantages of worrying'.

Sometimes just completing a chart like the one on the previous page can help you realise just how many disadvantages to worrying there really are.

It can also be very useful to look at the evidence for your belief in the benefits of worrying. Ask yourself the following questions:

- Do I have any evidence for my belief that worrying is helpful?
- If so, is it possible that there might be an alternative explanation?
- Do I have any evidence against my belief that worrying is helpful?
- Can I think of any times in my life when I didn't worry and my health was fine?
- Does worrying really prevent me from becoming ill? Or make good health more likely? Does

worrying have any effect at all on the likelihood of me having a serious health problem?
• What are the real effects of worrying – how is it affecting my life?

Using these questions, you can carry out another exercise based on gathering and comparing evidence, this time the evidence for and against your positive belief about worrying. First, write down your belief or thought about the positive effects of worrying. Then, underneath this, write down two column headings: 'Evidence that supports this belief' and 'Evidence that does not support this belief'. List all the evidence you can come up with under each heading.

Test it out: try not worrying!

If you've read this section on 'superstitious beliefs' and still aren't convinced, then maybe you should try not worrying and see what happens!

Many people who hold positive beliefs about worrying have difficulty stopping worrying, mainly because they're afraid of what will happen if they stop. Will they tempt fate? Will they find out that something is seriously wrong with their health? Will they be unable to cope? One of the best ways to find out whether worrying is really helping is to stop it and see what happens. Why not try the following experiment?

- For one day, keep worrying. Record what happens throughout the day. Also record how anxious you feel on a scale of 0–100 per cent.

- The next day, don't worry. Give yourself permission to let the worries go. Record what happens throughout the day. Also make a note of how anxious you feel on a scale of 0–100 per cent.

- Keep alternating days of worry and no worry for a week or two. Then compare your records for 'worry days' and 'no worry days'. Ask yourself – did worrying really keep you healthy? Did your 'no worry days' result in bad news about your health? How did worrying affect your anxiety levels? Write down how you felt. After you've done this, you may want to go back and add to your responses in the 'Weighing the Evidence' section (page 57).

You have now considered the advantages and the disadvantages of worrying, and weighed the evidence for and against your belief(s) about the positive effects of worrying. Using all of this information, you may be able to come up with a new, more realistic thought or belief about the effects of worrying. For example, a belief that 'If I stop worrying about my health I am tempting fate' could be replaced with 'Worrying does not really protect my health – it just makes me anxious and I feel terrible. If I stop worrying it won't have an impact on my health'.

Try to write out an alternative, more realistic belief about the effect of worrying.

Remind yourself about this new belief whenever you find yourself worrying.

7

Reducing Your Focus on the Body

Learning to pay your body less attention

We've discussed why constantly checking physical symptoms can actually increase anxiety levels. Remember that your body goes through natural and normal changes every day, so too much focus on the body will result in you noticing even the most minor change. These changes provide very little useful information in terms of detecting illness because they're so often harmless and downright ordinary. But if you focus too much on these changes they can start to make you worry, and then as you worry you get more anxious, which can produce even more physical changes, which makes you even more preoccupied with checking your body and you worry more ... producing a vicious circle.

An experiment with focusing on physical symptoms

If you still aren't convinced that too much focus on your symptoms may be making the problem worse, try the following experiment:

1. Give a physical symptom that is bothering you a severity rating from 0–10.
2. Spend five minutes thinking about nothing but the physical symptom that's concerning you. Keep all your attention on the symptom.
3. At the end of five minutes, write down what happened to the symptom. Did it get worse? Better? Give it a rating from 0–10.
4. Spend five minutes doing something else completely different. For example, try taking a piece of paper and writing down, in detail, what the room you're sitting in looks like.
5. At the end of five minutes, write down what happened to the symptom. Did it get worse? Better? Give it a rating from 0–10.
6. Compare the ratings. What happened when you were concentrating on your symptom compared to when you concentrated on something else?

Many people find that their symptoms get more severe or that they notice them more when they are focusing on them. When they turn their attention to something else, they stop noticing the symptom or it seems to feel less intense. What does this tell you about focusing on your body's sensations?

Finding ways to distract yourself

Reducing the amount of focus on your body can be extremely helpful. But this isn't easy to do. If you try to force yourself to stop thinking about your symptoms, you'll probably find you think about them even more! It's more helpful if you find ways to distract yourself from focusing on your body.

Tips for distracting yourself

- Do something you enjoy. Perhaps go for a walk or a swim, or do some gardening or cooking. Reading a magazine or a book, emailing a friend, watching television, or listening to the radio may also be helpful.

- Do something engaging. Choose an activity that requires you to pay attention. Plan your next holiday, make a list of things to do, or do a crossword puzzle.

> Anything that will keep you occupied and your brain busy!
> * Think of a fun holiday you've had, or imagine your favourite place.
> * Talk to someone else. Get them to help distract you! If you need to, call a friend or family member. You don't need to tell them that you want them to distract you – as long as you talk about something other than your health, it may help take your mind off your worries.

It can be useful to keep track of your efforts using the daily diary for health anxiety (see page 68). This will help you monitor your progress.

Remember: You're not trying to get rid of physical symptoms. Although your symptoms might become less intense as your anxiety levels come down, physical changes and sensations are normal and aren't going to go away. Your goal should be to reduce your focus on these symptoms and how much you are worrying about them.

Reducing checking behaviours

Checking your body for signs of physical illness can

be useful, as long as it's not done to excess. For example, doctors recommend that women check monthly (not daily!) for lumps in their breasts. However, like focusing on your body, excessive checking can make you aware of even the smallest change or physical sensation. It also does a good job of keeping you preoccupied with worry. There's another problem with checking, too – poking, prodding, touching or squeezing a lump, bump or blemish can make it swollen and sore, and the chances are that this will make you even more worried!

Reducing checking behaviours is one of the most helpful ways to lessen the focus on your body and to move your attention away from your worry. Most people find it quite hard to stop checking, at least at first, but it tends to get a lot easier after even a little while.

How do you check your body?

A useful first step is to think of all of the different ways you check your body. Some people check for lumps and bumps with their fingers; others examine their mouths, throats or eyes in the mirror; others measure their pulse; others weigh themselves; and others poke and prod to see if they feel any pain. And those are just a few examples! In your notebook, on a sheet of paper, or on your computer or smartphone, write down all of the different ways you check your body.

How to stop checking

The next step is to stop checking. You may want to tackle this in stages if it feels too overwhelming to get rid of them all at once. You'll very likely feel tempted to check, but try your best to resist the urge. It's important to remember that reducing your checking behaviours will probably make you more worried and anxious at first – but remember: reducing checking behaviour will help you feel much better in the long run.

If you struggle to resist the urge to check your body, then try the following exercise for a few days:

1. Set aside five minutes sometime during the day, preferably in the late afternoon or early evening, to check your body. Stick to that time every day.
2. Whenever you have the urge to check, postpone the checking by telling yourself that you have some time later in the day when you are allowed to check. If you do feel very anxious when you

resist checking, it might be helpful to use some of the distraction strategies discussed earlier.

3. When the time arrives, and only if you feel it necessary to do so, you can check your body for a maximum of five minutes (use a timer).

4. If, however, you get to your checking time and you have no pressing need to check yourself, then don't check your body. Only use the checking time if the urge to do so is strong, and then make sure you stop when your time is up.

5. If you go without using your checking time, then you must wait until the following day's checking time before you allow yourself to check your body again.

Once you are able to confine your checking to the short checking time every day, then make your checking time every second or third day. Do this until you are able to resist the urge to check almost all of the time. By this stage you should be able to check your body no more often than is reasonable.

If you're unsure about how much checking is reasonable, ask around. You can ask your GP for advice, or check with family or friends to see how frequently they check their bodies. It might be useful for you to keep track of your efforts to reduce checking behaviour and your level of anxiety. You can use a diary like the one on page 37 to keep track of how you're doing.

8

Reducing Your Focus on Illness

Seek reassurance less often

What's wrong with seeking reassurance?

Sometimes it is appropriate to seek advice about your health. If you feel ill or notice an unusual change in your body, it's often a good idea to consult a doctor or mention the symptom to a friend or family member. Having a doctor tell you that there's nothing to worry about, or talking over worries with friends and family, can be very reassuring.

However, sometimes reassurance-seeking can become a major problem if you do it too much. When this happens, the comfort provided by reassurance doesn't last and you may start questioning what the doctor or your loved ones have said. This often leads to the need for more and more reassurance. And that's not all – like focusing on your body and excessive checking, reassurance-seeking keeps you preoccupied with your health and worrying.

In the long run, for people with health anxiety, reassurance does not work. Most of the time, it makes things even worse.

How do you stop seeking reassurance?

First of all, when you feel worried about your health, try not to ask for advice or comfort from anyone else. You might even want to talk to your friends and family about this decision before you take action – let them know that if you do ask for reassurance, they should help you by not giving it.

Perhaps you could ask them to change the subject if you ask, or remind you that you made an agreement that they wouldn't answer you. Even though this will very likely help you tremendously in the long run, in the short term it may make you feel more anxious. Be prepared to use your distraction strategies (page 79).

Keep a record of how often you ask for reassurance or talk about your health – you can use the diary on page 37. If you aren't given reassurance, you will discover that you gradually ask for it less often, and start to feel less worried. Keep in mind that seeking reassurance from friends and family members can happen in various ways – you may ask about the meaning of symptoms (for example, 'I noticed this spot on my skin. What do you think it is?', or comparing your symptoms to theirs (for example, 'I sometimes notice my heart fluttering, do you ever experience that?', or asking them to check your symptoms (for example, 'Can you look at this spot on my arm again? Do you think it has changed?' All of these are forms of reassurance seeking.

Spend less time finding out about illness

Why does finding out about illness make you more anxious?

Spending time finding out about illness, as we discussed earlier, is bound to make you feel more anxious. First, it can make you more aware of every symptom and change in your body. You may even find symptoms you hadn't noticed before, especially if you start looking for them.

Second, even reliable medical information is easily misinterpreted by people who don't have medical training. Many common, non-specific symptoms are shared by a wide range of conditions, from those that you need not worry about to those rare cases that are life-threatening. The trouble is that much of the information that you might find on the Internet and elsewhere creates the impression that dreaded diseases are more common than they really are, which causes people to overestimate their risk and make the mistake of thinking that they do have a serious illness. If you spend time finding out about illness you may be tempted to try to diagnose yourself. This is a big mistake if you are not a doctor! You'll probably reach the wrong conclusion and cause yourself unnecessary anxiety.

Third, not all the information you will read is reliable, and so the more you look for information, the more likely you are to encounter conflicting advice. This creates doubt about the medical advice you have been given, which can exacerbate your anxiety, and increase your desire to continue combing through any information you can find.

Despite the fact that using the Internet or other resources to find out more about physical symptoms and related causes tends to significantly increase anxiety, many people find themselves spending a large amount of time engaged in this activity. It is not uncommon for people with health anxiety to spend hours on the Internet researching their symptoms. Even though they may realise it makes them feel worse, they find themselves doing it over and over again.

In general, for the above reasons, seeking medical information online or through other avenues (aside from consulting a doctor) tends to exacerbate anxiety rather than relieve it. However, even if you do find some comfort through this form of reassurance seeking, remember that it is short-lived! You will likely find that it is not long before you have the urge to check again ... and the vicious circle continues.

How to stop finding out about illness

If you're someone who spends a lot of time researching illness, now is the time to stop. Stop reading medical books or encyclopedias and stop looking up your symptoms on the Internet. If you use the Internet to find information, delete your browser history and bookmarks that you use to go to medical sites. If you're somebody who watches medical programmes on television and reads the health sections of magazines and newspapers, then think about cutting back on these activities. This may increase your worry in the short term – but remember, it will help decrease your worry in the long term.

When you feel the urge to 'research', use distraction to help take your mind off it (page 79). If you need to, ask your friends and family to remind you to stop.

Again, it's useful to record your progress using a daily diary for health anxiety like the one on page 37.

What if you are not convinced that finding out about illness is feeding your anxiety? You might find it helpful to do an experiment to find out. Here are a few ways to test the hypothesis that finding out about your illness is making you feel worse, not better:

1. The next time you get the urge to do some health research, go ahead and do it. However, before you start, rate your anxiety on a scale of 0–10 (0 = no anxiety, 10 = high anxiety). Engage in the activity of finding out about your illness for 30 minutes. Then rate your anxiety again. Did your anxiety go up or down?

    Continue with this for one week. Every time you want to spend time researching your physical symptoms, go ahead and do so, but rate your anxiety before and after. Keep a record of your ratings.

    At the end of the week, review your before and after ratings, and look at how many times you engaged in activities related to finding out about your illness.

    What does this information tell you? Did your anxiety go up or down as a result of researching your symptoms? How many times – and how much time overall – are you spending on this activity? Based on this information, how do you think finding out about illness is impacting your anxiety levels?

2. Compare finding out about illness with not finding out about illness. There are a couple of ways of doing this.

   a. The next time you get the urge to do some health research, go ahead and do it. Before you start, rate your anxiety on a scale of 0–10 (0 = no anxiety, 10 = high anxiety). Engage in the activity of finding out about your illness for 30 minutes. Then rate your anxiety again. Did your anxiety go up or down?

   Here's the twist – after this first step is complete, the very next time you get the urge to do some health research – DON'T! Instead, rate your anxiety on a scale of 0–10, just like you did the first time. Then engage in a distracting activity to help take your mind off it (see page 79). After 30 minutes, rate your anxiety again. Did your anxiety go up or down?

   How do you think finding out about illness is impacting your anxiety about your health?

   b. You can also try this over a longer period. For example, you could continue finding out about illness as you normally do over a period of one week. Each day, at the end of the day, rate your overall anxiety level for the day using the 0–10 scale. The following week, do not engage in any activity that involves finding out about illness or researching your symptoms. Again, at the end of each day, rate your overall anxiety level for the day using the 0–10 scale. At the end of the two-week period, review your results. Did you feel better or worse when you did not engage in health research?

How do you think finding out about illness is impacting your anxiety about your health?

Stop avoiding information about illness

Avoidance keeps anxiety going

Just as some people spend too much time finding out about illness (and need to stop looking for information), other people avoid any information at all about health (or their feared illness) because it increases their anxiety. If you're one of the many who avoid health information, you may, for example, find that you purposely avoid TV programmes about your feared illness, or avoid reading articles on health in the newspapers or magazines. This kind of avoidance can decrease anxiety in the short term. But what about the long term? Avoidance tends to keep anxiety going. It prevents you from learning to think rationally about your health. As long as you keep avoiding information about illness, you'll continue to feel anxious and upset whenever you do hear or read anything about illness. So what can you do?

How to stop avoiding information about illness

The key is to stop avoiding information about illness. This can be done gradually, at your own pace. A good way to start is to make a list of all of the situations or sources of information that you've been avoiding due to fear of getting anxious or upset about your health. Rate each item on your list in terms of how anxious you think it would make you (0 represents not anxious at all and 10 represents very anxious). Look at how Mary ranked the situations she would usually avoid:

What I have avoided	Anxiety rating
Watching TV programmes about cancer	10
Reading articles about cancer in the newspaper or in magazines	8
Listening to other people talk about cancer	6

Using the table below, make a list of the sources of information about health and illness that make you anxious about your health and that you prefer to avoid. Then rate each one according to how anxious you think you would be if you were in that situation. If you need more space, copy the table into your notebook, computer or smartphone.

What I have avoided	Anxiety rating (0–10)
1	
2	
3	

You may need to spend some time to adjust your list as you think more about the things that make you anxious and break down some of the difficult ones into easier steps.

Graded exposure

The next step is to get ready to start confronting the things you listed that you usually try to avoid. The best way to confront these is to tackle the ones that make you the least anxious and work up to the ones that make you the most anxious. This is known as graded exposure.

Facing up to the things on your list will probably make you feel anxious. However, the longer you're able to stay in the situation, the less anxious you'll eventually start to feel, because you are showing your brain that it needn't make you anxious. This is known as desensitisation.

Mary started this exercise by finding ways to listen to other people talking about cancer. She stopped herself from walking away when she heard other people talking about health or illness, and even asked her husband or a friend to talk to her about cancer. At first, she attempted to stay in the conversation for five minutes, and then moved up to ten minutes. When this started to feel manageable, she decided to read a short article on cancer in the newspaper, and then tried a longer one. And so on, until many of the things that she had been avoiding stopped making her so anxious. What helped for Mary to face her feared situations was to challenge her worrying thoughts using the techniques described in Chapter 6 (page 61).

Recording your graded exposure

Now that your list is ready and you are ready to face these situations, you should copy them into the table overleaf, in order from least to most anxiety, with a rating of how anxious you expect each one to make you feel in the second column.

In turn, confront each one, and record how anxious you are at first. Is the actual anxiety as bad as you expected? Stay in the situation, if you can, until your anxiety has come down to, at most, 2 or 3 on your scale. Don't be put off by setbacks; keep at it until the situations don't frighten you so much. Reward yourself for your successes.

Reducing other kinds of avoidance

Avoiding physical activity

Are you avoiding physical activity? Are you sitting or lying down whenever you notice a particular symptom? A big problem with stopping or cutting down on your normal activities is that it makes you less fit, and this in turn can make you feel tired and unwell. Then, when you do try to exert yourself, you'll feel even worse – not because you are ill, but because you are less fit. Fatigue and breathlessness, as well as muscle aches and pains, happen very easily

Situation	Expected anxiety 0–10	Anxiety rating at the start 0–10	Anxiety rating at the end 0–10

when you're unfit, but if you have difficulties with health anxiety, you may misinterpret these as signs of illness, leading you to reduce your activity levels even more – and so the vicious circle continues.

Also, remember that physical activity is a useful way of managing stress and is good for our moods. We noted in Chapter 2 that stress can be a trigger for health anxiety, and can make health and other types of anxiety harder to manage. So if you feel more stressed or less happy, then your health anxiety might worsen – another vicious circle and another reason to resume physical activity!

So, if you have cut down on or stopped physical activity, it's important that you start moving again. If you have been inactive for quite a while, remember that you won't be able to do as much as you once could, at least at first. You'll have to ease back into it.

Avoiding the doctor

While many people with health anxiety make multiple trips to the doctor, or even see multiple doctors, about their physical symptoms and health concerns, other people with health anxiety do the opposite: they avoid going to the doctor at all, even for check-ups. When a medical test is ordered, they don't get it. This is a good example of avoidance.

People with health anxiety may avoid going to the doctor or undergoing medical tests because they are afraid of what they will find out. This strategy serves to increase anxiety over the long run. While it is not helpful to repeatedly ask your doctor for medical reassurance, it is also not helpful to do the opposite and never go to the doctor at all. It is reasonable and good practice to attend your regular check-ups and talk about health concerns you may have with your doctor – but only when necessary.

How do you know when it is necessary to go to the doctor and when it is not? You might want to consider meeting with your family doctor to talk about your health anxiety. Explain that you are trying to reduce your anxiety about your health and that part of this involves only coming to the doctor when necessary. Ask your doctor for suggestions regarding how to decide whether a medical appointment is needed. The answer to this question will probably vary from person to person, depending on their age and medical history. You may find it helpful to establish clear guidelines with your doctor about when to make an appointment (e.g., yearly check-up, to receive a prescription renewal, if you experience a significant change to a pre-existing condition, or if you experience new symptoms that last for a period that you and your doctor agree on). Some doctors may suggest a 'two-week rule' for symptoms connected to the health anxiety – wait two weeks before making an appointment, because many symptoms reduce or clear up on their own within that time period.

How to resume activities you have been avoiding

If you have difficulty resuming some of your activities, list the activities you have been avoiding in the table overleaf, or, if you need more space, copy it into your notebook or onto your computer or smartphone. You can either rank them in terms of how much physical effort they require or, if you think it might make things easier, how anxious you will feel when you do the activity. Start with the easiest item on the list, and once you feel comfortable with that, you can begin to work your way up to the more challenging activities.

It is often helpful to reward yourself for resuming these activities, though the activities themselves might be all the reward you need.

Keep at it until you feel that you have reclaimed your life from your health anxiety. Setbacks are normal; just try again. You may want to use a daily diary for health anxiety (see page 37 to keep track of your progress).

Activity	Physical effort or anxiety (0–10)

9

Summing It Up

This book has provided you with information about health anxiety, and set out practical ways in which you can help reduce this anxiety. Unfortunately, there's no 'quick fix' for health anxiety. Overcoming it takes a lot of work. You may have to practise the techniques repeatedly to get the hang of them.

Keep a record of your progress (you can use the daily diary of health anxiety on page 37) so that you can look back at what has happened as you complete more and more of the exercises. Remember that challenging your thoughts about illness can be very helpful in its own right, but it's also a skill you can use when you're trying the other exercises.

Don't worry if you don't feel better immediately – it might be a little while before you start noticing improvement. You may also experience some 'bad spells' when your anxiety levels increase but don't get discouraged – 'ups and downs' are normal. When you do notice an increase in anxiety, consider it an opportunity to practise the techniques you have learned from this manual.

Many people find it helpful to summarise what they have learned about coping with health anxiety. You may have noticed that some of the exercises were more helpful than others, or that there were particular ways of challenging your worries about illness that were really effective. You may find it useful to write down what has been most useful for you in your notebook. Refer to this list whenever you find yourself struggling with health anxiety in the future.

Other Things that Might Help

This book has provided you with an introduction to the problems caused by health anxiety and what you can do to overcome them. Some people will find that this is all they need to do to see a big improvement, while others may feel that they need a bit more information and help, and in that case there are some longer and more detailed self-help books around. Using self-help books, particularly those based on CBT, has been found to be particularly effective in the treatment of anxiety problems. Ask your GP if there's a 'Books on Prescription' scheme running in your area – if there isn't, we recommend the following books:

Overcoming Health Anxiety by Rob Willson and David Veale, published by Robinson

It's Not All in Your Head: How Worrying About Your Health Could Be Making You Sick – And What You Can Do About It by Gordon Asmundson and Steven Taylor, published by Routledge Mental Health and Guilford Press

Stop Worrying About Your Health! by George Zgourides, published by New Harbinger

Understanding Health Anxiety by Christine Küchemann and Diana Sanders, published by Oxford Cognitive Therapy Centre (OCTC) (www.octc.co.uk/)

The following books deal with more general anxiety problems and you might find them useful as well:

Overcoming Anxiety by Helen Kennerley, published by Robinson

The Anxiety and Phobia Workbook by Edmund J. Bourne, published by New Harbinger

Sometimes the self-help approach works better if you have someone supporting you. Ask your GP if there's anyone at the surgery who would be able to work through your self-help book with you. Some surgeries have Graduate Mental Health Workers who would be able to help in this way, or who might offer general support. He or she is likely to be able to spend more time with you than your GP and may be able to offer follow-up appointments.

For some people a self-help approach may not be enough. If this is the case for you, don't despair – there are other kinds of help available.

Talk to your GP – make an appointment to talk through the different treatment options on offer to you. Your GP can refer you to an NHS therapist for Cognitive Behavioural Therapy – most places now have CBT available on the NHS, although there can be a considerable waiting list. Don't be put off if you've not found working through a CBT-based self-help manual right for you – talking to a therapist can make a big difference. If an NHS therapist isn't available in your area or you'd prefer not to wait to see one, ask your GP to recommend a private therapist.

Although CBT is widely recommended for anxiety problems there are many other kinds of therapy available that you could also discuss with your GP.

Medication can be very helpful for some people and sometimes a combination of medication and psychological therapy can work wonders. However, you need to discuss this form of treatment and any possible side-effects with your doctor to work out whether it's right for you.

The following organisations offer help and advice on anxiety problems and you may find them a useful source of information:

Anxiety Care UK
Tel: 07552 877219
Email: admin@anxietycare.org.uk and
recoveryinfo@anxietycare.org.uk
Website: www.anxietycare.org.uk

British Association for Behavioural &
Cognitive Psychotherapies (BABCP)
Tel: 0161 705 4304
Email: babcp@babcp.com
Website: www.babcp.com
Provides contact details for therapists in your area,
both NHS and private.

Mind
Tel: 020 8519 2122
Website: www.mind.org.uk